sources from the ancient near east

volume 1, fascicle 4

hittite birth rituals:
an introduction

by

Gary Beckman

undena publications

malibu 1978

SOURCES AND MONOGRAPHS ON THE ANCIENT NEAR EAST

Editors: Giorgio Buccellati, Marilyn Kelly-Buccellati

Assistant Editor: Patricia Oliansky

These two series make available original documents in English translation (Sources) and important studies by modern scholars (Monographs) as a contribution to the study of the history, religion, literature, art, and archaeology of the Ancient Near East. Inexpensive and flexible in format, they are meant to serve the specialist by bringing within easy reach basic publications, often in updated versions, to provide imaginative education outlets for undergraduate and graduate courses, and to reach interested segments of the educated lay audience.

Hittite Birth Rituals: An Introduction
Gary Beckman

This article presents an outline of procedures followed by the ancient Hittite woman in dealing with the processes of pregnancy and birth. These ritual texts with notes and comments include translations of seven relevant incantations dealing with pregnancy, delivery, and ceremonies following parturition. Magico-religious, medical, festal observances relating to the birth cycle are included. Philological details are kept to a minimum for the sake of the non-specialist while scholars in the field will find ample documentation in the author's dissertation.

© 1978 by Undena Publications, P.O. Box 97, Malibu, California 90265

Second printing with minor corrections, 1982

ISBN: 0-89003-003-0

PREFACE

Birth constitutes the first of life's crises, one which many individuals, especially in cultures without modern gynecological and surgical knowledge, do not survive. Birth is also the beginning of a life, and in the view of many peoples, determinative for the future course of that life. Therefore it is not surprising that the Hittites, who devoted a great deal of energy to the creation of rituals for various problems, life crises, and events, should have included many texts dealing with birth in their ritual corpus.

This monograph presents an outline of procedures followed by the Hittites in dealing with the processes of birth and pregnancy, as well as translations of seven of the relevant texts. These seven rituals are the best preserved and most understandable of those edited, with philological commentary, in my 1977 Yale University dissertation, "Hittite Birth Rituals." In general the notes and comments accompanying the translations in the present work provide only the information necessary to facilitate the understanding of the non-specialist. Philologists seeking justification for particular renderings are referred to my dissertation, although in a number of instances the translations given here have been slightly revised since the completion of that work.

In the translations, the units of text set off by horizontal strokes on the tablets have been indicated as modern paragraphs. Line numbers have been given only for the first line of a paragraph; numbers followed by an apostrophe (e.g., 7') are employed in instances where, the beginning of the column of text having been lost, numeration has accordingly begun with the first preserved line. The sigla employed are: square brackets [ ], enclosing textual material destroyed on the surface of the tablet and restored by the editor; round brackets ( ), enclosing words and phrases not present in the text but necessary for a clear and idiomatic rendering into English; and pointed brackets < >, enclosing words or signs mistakenly omitted by the ancient scribe.

ABBREVIATIONS

ABoT	*Ankara Arkeoloji Müzesinde bulunan Boğazköy Tabletleri* (1948).
JAOS	*Journal of the American Oriental Society.*
JNES	*Journal of Near Eastern Studies.*
KBo	*Keilschrifttexte aus Boghazköi* (1916-23; 1954-).
KUB	*Keilschrifturkunden aus Boghazköi* (1921-).
MDOG	*Mitteilungen der Deutschen Orient-Gesellschaft zu Berlin.*
MSS	*Münchener Studien zur Sprachwissenschaft.*
RLA	*Reallexikon der Assyriologie* (1928-38; 1957-).
THeth	*Texte der Hethiter* (1971-).

TABLE OF CONTENTS

A. INTRODUCTION

From the many hundreds of ritual tablets and fragments uncovered in the excavations of the ancient Hittite capital of Ḫattuša (modern Boghazköy), more than twenty different compositions dealing with birth, some of them attested in several copies, have thus far been identified.[1] In utilizing the evidence of these texts to construct a schema of Hittite practice in regard to pregnancy and birth, it must be kept in mind that the details of this schema may be only distantly related to what actually took place in the households of the common people.[2] It is quite probable that most women gave birth without elaborate ceremony, either during pregnancy or during parturition—certainly the expenditures entailed in the carrying out of rituals such as those described, for example, in Text 7, were beyond the means of the ordinary family.

Also, the birth rituals themselves do not present a unified corpus, but rather detail procedures from various population groups,[3] areas,[4] and periods within the history of the Hittite state.[5] All of these ritual texts were probably brought to Ḫattuša, and in most cases recopied there over the course of years, in order that the knowledge contained in them might be accessible to those practitioners who served the royal family in times of crisis. It was of no consequence that contradictory practices were found in the rituals as a group; what was important was that the experts who aided the ladies of the royal harem in problems of reproduction have available to them as much information as possible. Therefore it is doubtful that all of the procedures included in the following outline were carried out in the case of any single pregnancy, even where these procedures are not mutually exclusive.

1. Pre-parturition

The very entering of a woman into the state of pregnancy could be marked by a special festival performed in honor of the Mother-goddesses (Text 7 Obv. 44-46).

During pregnancy, monthly rites might be carried out for these same deities (Text 7 Obv. 47-50), and the mother-to-be was subject to certain restrictions in her diet (Text 7 Obv. 17-19) and sexual relations (Text 7 Obv. 5, Rev. 3-4). At various times during pregnancy offerings (Text 7 Obv. 6-9, Rev. 5-9, 20-24) and purifications (Text 7 Obv. 10-13, Rev. 35-36) were made, and after a certain point, the woman could

---

[1] For a complete list, see G. Beckman, "Hittite Birth Rituals," Diss. Yale University 1977, pp. 384-85.

[2] See H. Hoffner, *JNES* 27 (1968), 203, where it is shown that there exists a discrepancy between naming practices as described in Hittite mythological texts and actual usage as revealed by the corpus of personal names.

[3] For instance, Text 4 contains Hattic incantations, while Text 5 and Text 6 are derived from Hurro-Luwian sources.

[4] For example, to judge from the probable location of the cities named in the incantation in Text 1, this text is of central Anatolian origin, while Obv. 38 and Rev. 46 of Text 7 indicate quite clearly a southern provenience.

[5] For example, Text 3 may go back to an Old Hittite original, Text 5 entered Hatti during the Middle Hittite period, and the ritual preserved on the reverse of KUB XLIV 4 + KBo XIII 241 is very late in composition.

be separated from her family for the duration of her term (Text 7 Obv. 14-16, 20-23). It seems, however, that in the majority of cases births occurred in the home.[6]

Prior to delivery an oracle might be sought to determine if the woman was in the proper moral condition to successfully give birth (Text 7 Rev. 15-18), and offerings could be performed to correct the situation if the answer to this inquiry was negative (Text 7 Rev. 19-20).

Finally, there were rites to prepare the possessions of the woman (Text 7 Obv. 24-26, Rev. 28-30), the birth apparatus (Text 5, Text 7 Rev. 31-33) and the woman herself (Text 7 Rev. 35) for the act of parturition.

2. Parturition

The equipment necessary for delivery consisted of two stools and three cushions (Text 1 Obv. 1-4), or of two footstools (Text 2 i 5'-7') or, in texts of the Hurro-Luwian milieu, of the birth-stool (*harnau-*[7]—Text 5, Text 6, Text 7). If the apparatus developed a flaw during labor, this was considered to be a bad omen, and time permitting, the place of birth was changed (Text 6 i 7-11).

Various incantations to aid in delivery are attested: "The Incantation of Wailing" (Text 2 i 9'-12'), known only by title, takes its name from a characteristic activity of the mother during parturition and was presumably held to comfort her in the face of labor pains. The Hattic "Incantation of Blood" (Text 4 ii 1) and "Incantation of the Wind" (Text 4 ii 7) were intended to give aid in event of physical difficulties in delivery. In Text 1 (Obv. 9ff.) and in KUB XLIV 4 + KBo XIII 241 (Rev. 1ff.) mythological parallels are adduced to aid in parturition, while KBo XII 112 Rev. 8'ff. contains charms to induce the child to leave the body of the mother.

In regard to physical activities, we learn only that a substitute ewe might be brought in for the mother (Text 2 i 18'-24') and that the new-born child fell into a receiving blanket (Text 1 Obv. 7).

More elaborate rites which could be carried out at the time of birth were "The Festival of Birth" for the Mother-goddesses (Text 7 Obv. 51-55), "The Festival of the Womb" (Text 7 Obv. 37-39, Rev. 45-46, KBo VII 74 ii 4'), "The Festival of Wailing" (KBo VII 74 ii 4') and "The Festival of the Pigeons" (KBo VII 74 ii 3'). These last three festivals were all performed in honor of the Hurrian goddess Šaušga, a figure quite similar to the Mesopotamian Ištar. Unfortunately we learn little about these rites beyond their names.

Finally, Text 7 Obv. 40-41 seems to prescribe a period of peace within the family or group of the mother immediately after the birth.

3. Post-parturition

It is in this area that the weight of the material preserved in the Hittite birth rituals falls. The most widely attested of the rites performed immediately following birth is an incantation seeking to remove

---

[6]This is the impression given by Text 5, in which the "inner chamber" so often mentioned was probably the bedroom of the expectant parents. Compare also Text 6, where the birth-stool was apparently originally set up in the home of the mother.

[7]See below, Text 5, Note 3.

evil from the new-born and/or to secure a favorable fate for the child (Text 2 iv 7′-12′, Text 3 Rev. 2′-10′, 18′-21′, KBo XVII 60 Rev. 5′-11′, KUB XLIV 4 + KBo XIII 241 Rev. 22-34, 771/f).

At this time there might also be performed a ceremony to ensure the continued fertility of the mother (Text 2 iv 13′-18′), or a rite to confer the proper sexual role upon the new-born (Text 2 iv 13′-18′). A determination of the fate of the child was also possible (Text 3 Obv. 10-15, KBo XII 112 Obv. 11′?).

In addition, we find purificatory rites for the mother (Text 3 Obv. 20-21, KUB XLIV 4 + KBo XIII 241 Rev. 15, KUB XLIV 58 iii 7′), the birth equipment (Text 6 i 18-57, ii 1-6) and the child (Text 3 Obv. 10-19, Rev. 7′-17′, Bo 4951).

These purificatory rites might be performed at various times in the days and months after the child had entered the world—on the second night (Text 6 ii 5), the fourth night (Text 6 Col. iv) or the seventh day (Text 7 Obv. 28-29, Rev. 38-39, Bo 4951 Rev. 17′ff.). Finally, a male child might undergo a final purification after three months had passed (Text 7 Obv. 31-33, Rev. 41-42), while a baby girl could experience this ceremony only after four months (Text 7 Obv. 34-36, Rev. 43-44).

4. Character of the Activity

It is immediately apparent that the great majority of the activities listed here fall into a realm more accurately described as magico-religious than as medical. The exceptions to this generalization are few and uncertain: KBo VIII 130 possibly prescribes the administering of drugs to a pregnant woman, yet refers to itself in its colophon as an incantation (*ŠI-PÀT*). Text 3 Obv. 23 speaks of the giving of "fresh medicine" to the new-born, but the context is not entirely comprehensible. Finally, the numerous purifications of the child might well have been of hygienic value, and the substance *kunzigannaḫit*[8] often employed in these purifications was possibly a drug.

This preponderant concern with the magico-religious, almost to the exclusion of the medical, sets the Hittite birth rituals in sharp contrast to available Mesopotamian materials dealing with birth.[9] Many of these latter texts also contain magico-religious elements, but the majority also present instructions for the preparation and administering of medications in the form of potions, salves, poultices, enemas, etc.

That the absence of true medicine in the Hittite birth rituals is not merely the result of the chance of discovery is suggested by a royal letter, 652/f + 28/n + 127/r, sent by Ramses II of Egypt to Ḫattušili III of Hatti, and recently published by E. Edel.[10] In this communication the Egyptian first refers to an earlier request of the Hittite monarch:

> [That which my brother] wrote t[o me concerning] Mata[n]az[i],
> his [sis]ter: "Let my brother send a man, so that medicines
> might be prepared for her, so that she might be caused to give
> birth!" (Obv. 8-13)

Ramses then adds his reply:

> Look, Matanazi, the sister of my brother—(I), the King, your
> brother, know (of) her. It is said (in your letter) that she

---

[8]See below, Text 7, Note 3.

[9]See R. Labat, *RLA*, III, 177ff., for a convenient summary.

[10]*Ägyptische Ärzte und ägyptische Medizin am hethitischen Königshof* (Opladen, 1976), pp. 67ff.

is a fifty-year-old. No—she is a sixty-year-old! . . . No—
for a woman who has completed sixty years, it is not possible
to prepare medicines for her, so that she might still be caused
to give birth. (Obv. 16-Rev. 5)

The pharaoh concludes by agreeing nonetheless to send the requested expert and materials in the hope that divine intervention might bring about a miracle in this instance (Rev. 6-13).

It is the Hittite attitude which is of interest here. If there were persons at the Hittite court who were expert in the use of medicines in the treatment of gynecological problems, they would certainly have informed Ḫattušili that his hopes in regard to the possible fertility of his sister were misplaced.

We are led to conclude that the Hittite practitioners had no real practical acquaintance with the use of medicines in gynecology, and thus no understanding of their capacities and limitations. This conclusion, drawn from a text of a different type, supports our observations concerning the Hittite texts which deal specifically with human reproduction. That is, these works exhibit an almost exclusive reliance upon the magico-religious in their efforts to bring about the successful entry of a new human being into the world. They also endeavor to secure for the new-born his social and ritual integration into the community, as well as a happy fate.

B. TEXTS IN TRANSLATION

Text 1. KUB XXX 29

Obv. 1. [When] a woman is giving birth, then the midwife prepa[re]s the following: [Two sto]ols (and) three cushions (are prepared in such a way that) [on] each stool is placed one cushion.

4. And [on]e cushion is spread out between the stools on the ground. When the child begins to fall (i.e., to be born), [then] the woman seats herself on the stools. And the midwife holds the receiving blanket with (her) [ha]nd. [And] you[1] shall repeatedly conjure as [foll]ows:

9. To the [go]ds allotments are given. The Sun-goddess in Arinna[2] has [se]ated herself, and the Throne-goddess in Ḫarpiš likewise, and Ḫatepi<nu> in Maliluḫa likewise, the Protective Genius in Karaḫna likewise, the [awe]some Telepinu in Taw(i)niya likewise, and Ḫuzziya in Ḫakmiš likewise. But for the Mother-goddess there did not remain a place; so for her, man<kind> remained (as) a [pl]ace.[3]

CHARACTER: Fourteenth century copy of Middle Hittite text. Hattic forerunner?

Text 2. KBo XVII 62 + 63

Col. i 1'. [. . . on one side] and on the other side [. . .] sits. (On?) the ear[th? . . . .] Then the child [falls (i.e., is born)? . . . .]

5'. Two smal[l] footstools [they bring? .] And one footstool [is placed] in fr[ont] of the woman, while the other footstool [is placed] be[hind] her. [Then] the midwives[1] se[at] themselves.

9'. But while the woman cr[ies out in labor, then the midwife] conjures repeatedly "The Incantation of Cry[ing Out."] At the time when the woman [begins] to cr[y out in labor, then the midwife] conjures repeatedly. But from one? ablet [. . . .] And the tablets of incantation are sep[arate.[2]]

14'. But at the point when the woman be[gins] to cry out in labor, (then for) the child they have already made prior preparations. The ch[ild] in that month, on those days, will be b[orn.] And her (the mother) they have already prepared.

18'. But while the [wom]an is still crying out, then a ewe which has been prepared—either preg[nant] or not—into the inner chamber they drive. But when the woman gives bir[th] (and) the child is falling (i.e., being born), then this ewe (over) the woman, o[ver her head? ,] three times they swing. And the midwife meanwhile [s]peaks [as follows:]

25'. "Whatever [evils?] the woman [afflict?,] . . . her away [. . . .] [And] may [they] relea[se] the woman!"[3]

Col. iv 3'. "And to this [. . .]the <eter>nal rock sanctuary[4] [. . .] which down [. . .] keep in place!, and [. . . k]ee[p!]

7'. "And co[m]e! [As] the rock sanctuary the wind and ra[in] cannot [lift from] its place, down in these [. . .] he was born. And likewis[e] let [not] an evil thing lift [his life?] from its place! And let it likewise [be] protected! And let it be established for eternity!"

13'. And if a ma[le] child is then born, then the midwife th[us] speaks: "Loo[k!] Now I have brou[ght] the goods of a male child. But next y[ea]r I will certainly bring the goods of a female child!"[5]

16'. If it is a fema[le] child, then she speaks thus: "Now—look!--the goods [of a fema]le [child] I have brought. But next year the goods [of a ma]le [child] I will certainly bring!"

Colophon. [Tablet N[6]–"When] a Woman Gives Birth." Incomplete.[7] [Word (i.e., composition) of Tunaẖwiya,[8] the midwife.[9]

CHARACTER: Possibly a Middle Hittite tablet.

Comments and Notes to the Translation

COMMENT: The incantation beginning in line 9 attempts to deal with a real-life situation by establishing a connection between this situation and a mythological narrative. We are told that when the other deities had each received a city as a cult center, and none remained for the Mother-goddess, she was given the whole of mankind as her sphere of activity. In the context of the ritual, the taking of seats by the deities in their cult centers must be seen as parallel to the seating of the woman upon the stools. Presumably the lost lines of this text contained a request to the Mother-goddess to act favorably in connection with the birth occurring in the first two paragraphs.

NOTES:

[1] Addressed to either the midwife herself or to a ritual practitioner.

[2] This and the following cities were all located in the central Anatolian area inhabited by the Hattic people before the arrival of the Hittites. Similarly, all of the deities mentioned here belonged originally to the Hattians.

[3] After five very fragmentary lines, which probably continue the incantation begun in the preceding paragraph, the tablet is broken away. The reverse is uninscribed.

COMMENT: The preserved portion of this text deals specifically with parturition. In i 1'-8' the necessary apparatus and its positioning are detailed. i 9'-13' prescribe the recitation of a certain incantation to ease the pain of the mother in labor, and i 18' ff. describe a magical operation and an incantation for the moment of delivery. The obverse of the tablet breaks off in the middle of this incantation, and the preserved paragraphs of the reverse pick up again midway through an incantation on behalf of the child (iv 1'-12'), in which the permanence of rock is sought for his existence. Then a speech by the midwife seeking the continued fertility of the mother is presented (iv 13'-18'). The colophon informs us that the composition is not complete on this tablet. The activities probably continue with further purificatory rites on behalf of the child—cf. Text 7 Obv. 27-36, Rev. 39-44.

NOTES:

[1] The presence here of more than one midwife is unusual.

[2] Some of the incantations necessary for the carrying out of this ritual were inscribed on other tablets, a practice relatively rare at Boghazköy, but common in Mesopotamia.

[3] Col. i breaks off after one more fragmentary line. Cols. ii and iii having been entirely lost, the translation resumes with line 3' of Col. iv.

[4] The ^{NA4}hekur, "rock sanctuary," which played an important role in the royal funerary cult, was apparently a temple situated in a natural rock outcropping—see H. Otten, *MDOG* 94 (1963), 18ff., and H. G. Güterbock, *JNES* 26 (1967), 81.

[5] This is probably a reference to gifts given to the child at birth in rites intended to confer upon him the proper sexual role.

[6] In all probability this was the first tablet of the composition, but the possibility must be kept open that it was preceded by other tablets detailing the regimen for pregnancy.

[7] That is, the ritual is continued on another tablet.

[8] This may be the same woman attested as the author of a ritual for reproductive difficulties—see A. Goetze and E. H. Sturtevant, *The Hittite Ritual of Tunnawi* (New Haven, 1938).

[9] A few fragmentary lines follow before the tablet breaks off.

Text 3. KBo XVII 61[1]

Obv. i. [. . .] of her [wo]mb[?] [. . .] among which one is of wood [. . .] [on t]op l[ie.]

4. [. . . *hu*]*št*.[2] And here also one rennet is set. [. . .] fresh *taraša*.[3] [. . .] one small bronze knife (and) four bronze pegs.

7. [. . .] in [what]ever place I[4] shall bring up [the child, . . .] the diviner and the augur give. [. . .] the *ḫušt* (s)he swings overhead repeatedly.

10. [. . .] and to me the midwife [says: "A chil]d I, the midwife, have brought into the world!" [. . .] and when they hand the child over to me, [I do the following: When] I cleanse his mouth,[5] and he [is going to live, then] I give [him health[?].[6]] If he is not going to live, [then him I . . . .[7]] But the palace functionary stands [o]ver me when I cleanse his mouth.

16. [And the *taraš*]*a* I carry there, and the containers are placed. [And] the net is spread out. And the child on the containers with [. . .] I purify. The *taraša* I swing over him. [And] "wolf's head"[8] I burn up.

20. [And] I, the [Old] Woman[?],[9] wash her head, and the queen [in . . .] dresses her. But from that one I take away her own (clothes).[10] [And] I place the child on her[?] knees.

23. [. . . A]nd to him (the child) fresh medicine I have already given. But the medicine . . . [. . .] (s)he [. . . .] And I come (and) further, a copper box[?] (and[?]) medicine I give to him. [. . .] I take: cr[ocu]s[?], lettuce [. . .] (and) one + vessel(s) of cheap beer for drinking.

Rev. 2'.[11] [". . .]let him (i.e., some deity) chase (away)! [. . . sh]ort years, ditto # 3, [. . . di]tto # 4. But [to the mort]al (i.e., the child) may he [continually giv]e long year[s]! [. . .] May the Sun-goddess of the Earth[12] turn them into pebbles! [And away from him] let him/her take [them!"]

7'. [Then] I [. . .] and I conjure as follows: "Down from the sky it flowed. [. . . it flow]ed." And into the pen I went, and I requested a male goat from Immarni[13] [. . .] he[?] saw. But I, the Old Woman, with ten fingers [reach[?]] out, [and the male go]at I repeatedly hold against the mortal on (each of) the nine body parts:[14]

11'. [. . . e]yes are arranged against his eyes, eyebrow to eyebrow, ditto; [. . . ditto # 3;] ears to his ears, ditto # 4; mouths (*sic*!) to his mouth, ditto # 5; [liver to] liver, ditto # 6; gall bladder to gall bladder, ditto # 7; pelvis [to pelvis . . .] ditto # 8; anus to anus, ditto # 9; [. . . to] . . . , ditto # 10; testicles [to testicles, ditto # 11; kn]ee to knees, ditto; foot to foot, ditto. [. . .] . . . .

18'. [" . . .] to the high mountains he will carry off. [. . .] to the grass of the [Sun-god]dess [of the Earth] he will carry off. [. . .] let him [ta]ke[?], and let the male goat go to the Sun-goddess of the Earth! [. . .] to the Sun-goddess of the [Ea]rth let him hold a lighted torch!"[15]

22'. [. . .] the male goat I butcher. [. . .] I c[oo]k, and an image of wood [. . . these thi]ngs I burn up.[16]

CHARACTER: Middle Hittite copy of Old Hittite text.

Text 4. KUB XVII 28 ii 1-32

Col. ii 1. "Incantation of Blood"–When a woman is giv[ing birth] and her bleeding is inhibited, then [for her as follows] I conjure: (There follows an incantation in the as yet poorly understood Hattic language.)

7. "Incantation of the Wind"–When (a woman) is giving birth, and she does n[ot] break wind, then for her I con[jure] as follows: (Hattic)

CHARACTER: Thirteenth century copy of Hattic text from Middle Hittite period or earlier.

COMMENT: This text presents a post-parturition ritual in which activities are performed on behalf of both mother and child. Among the actions included here are a determination of the fate of the child, along with a mouth-washing ceremony (Obv. 10-15), the cleansing of the mother (Obv. 20-22), the invocation of the Sun-goddess of the Earth (Rev. 2'-6'), and a scapegoat ritual (Rev. 10'-24'). The emphasis in the preserved portions of the text is upon purification—both from physical uncleanness and from evil influences. The presence of the palace functionary in Obv. 15, taken together with that of the queen in Obv. 20, shows that this text, at least in its present form, was specifically intended for use in the royal family. That the queen herself does not give birth here, however, is demonstrated by the active role which she takes in the procedure soon after delivery.

NOTES:

[1] See H. Berman, *JAOS* 92 (1972), 466-68.

[2] Perhaps a mineral.

[3] This word is found in no other text, and its meaning cannot be deduced from its occurrences in this ritual.

[4] To judge from her activities in this line and in Obv. 22, the practitioner represented by the first person verbal forms in this text (outside of the quotation in Obv. 11) was probably a child's nurse. See H. Hoffner, *JNES* 27 (1968), 199ff., for the role of this occupation in Hittite texts.

[5] From the mucus present at birth.

[6] Apparently during the course of the mouth-washing operation a determination of the viability of the child was made. Whether this depended chiefly upon the child's physical condition or upon a divinatory act is uncertain, although the presence of the seer and augur in Obv. 8 points to the latter alternative.

[7] Unfortunately the verb denoting the action undertaken on or for the ill-fated child has been lost in the break. Since infanticide is attested in Hittite texts only in mythology (e.g., KBo XXII 2 Obv. 1-4), it is unlikely that such a drastic action is involved here.

[8] Probably a plant.

[9] The Sumerogram ^{SAL}SU.GI = Hittite $^{(SAL)}$ḫašauwa-, "Old Woman," is apparently a general term for a female ritual practitioner in Hittite texts.

[10] That is, the clothes of the mother, which had become soiled during birth.

[11] Only slight traces are visible in Rev. 1'.

[12] A chthonic deity often invoked to receive various evils into her realm, and to keep them penned up there where they could do no harm.

[13] A deity of the meadow and livestock, comparable to the Greek Pan.

[14] Nine is a standard number employed by the Hittites when referring to parts of the body, and in fact does not here correspond to the number of limbs and organs actually listed in Rev. 11'-16'. By means of the "matching ritual" here described, in which the body parts of the child are held against those of the goat, the evils present in the body of the former are ritually transferred to the latter. The evils are later disposed of once and for all along with the goat.

[15] That this incantation is only metaphorical, and that the goat is not actually driven off, is shown by Rev. 22' in which the animal is butchered.

[16] Only slight traces are preserved before the tablet breaks off.

COMMENT: Both bleeding and flatulence are normal preludes to delivery. Therefore the absence of either would be an ominous, if not indeed medically dangerous, sign. According to A. Kammerhuber's interpretation of the first difficult Hattic incantation (*MSS* 17 [1964], 26), these lines call upon the Storm-god to release his rain. This would be analogous to the hoped-for onset of bleeding in the woman.

Text 5. KUB IX 22 and Duplicates[1]

Col. ii 1.[2] [And] two jugs of wine he takes, (and) ab[ove . . . cedar,] tamarisk[?] (and) olive(-wood) [is bound on.] And one on this side, one on the other, he hangs.

4. And in whatever inner chamber the woman is, then outside of that inner chamber two pegs—one peg on one side and one on the other side—he poun[ds] (in). Further, on the pegs cedar, tamarisk[?] and olive (-wood) he binds.

9. A jug [. . .] (and) four[?] grape(-shaped) loaves are hu[ng] down. And the ball of yarn[?] one cuts[?] off in front.

12. And the chair, the table, the bed, the pot stand (and) the birth-stool[3] of the woman—and the woman herself—the *patili*-priest[4] swing[s] (over) with a sheldrake.[5]

15. And the woman in the inner chamber sacrifices on her own behalf for *zurgi*.[6] And she washes her hands. And one takes her in before the birth-stool.

18. And one duck to the path he sacrifices. But one duck to the *ḫabi* for *itkalziya* (and) *kulamušiya* he sacrifices. And the birth-stool and the pegs one b[in]ds (together).

22. And cedar, tamarisk[?] (and) olive(-woods) with red wool are bound up.[7] And the *patili*-priest takes them, and them on the woman, on the strap[?] (worn across her chest[?]) he places. And fine oil he pours on on her head,[8] and to her hand he binds red wool.

28. Further, the *patili*-priest takes the *ḫarnai*[9] out of the bowl, together with the cedar, tamarisk[?] (and) olive(-woods). And the mouth of the woman he purifies.

31. Then the *patili*-priest puts the bowl (and) the *ḫarnai* (therein) on the pegs, and it (the bowl) he covers up. Then the woman goes and to the birth-stool bows down. Further, (her) hand toward the birth-stool she holds out. Further, she seats herself, and her husband, the *patili*-priests and the *katra*-women[10] go, and they bow down to the woman.

38. And the *patili*-priest before the birth-stool makes a seal[ing] (of the chamber). But whatever *ḫarnai* in a measuring vessel was poured, and whichever two pegs outside, before the door of the inner chamber he pounds (in)—(these things he takes and) he puts the measuring vessel (of *ḫarnai*) on top and covers it up.

44. And to the *patili*-priests and *katra*-women they give to eat. And they go away. But when it becomes night (and) a star twinkles, then the *patili*-priest g[oe]s in and makes a (ritual-)opening (of the chamber) before the birth-stool.

Col. iii 1. And he bring[s] the woman inside. And she bows down before the birth-stool. [Fur]ther, she holds out (her) hand. Then from the inner chamber she comes forth, and the [*patil*]i-priest before the inner chamber makes a sealing.

6. [And] the woman sits down on the b[ed.] And near her [he]ad he places one wickerwork table. [Fur]ther, he places a *naḫiti*-loaf[11] (on it). And on the *naḫiti*[-loaf] the moon, the sun, and the star(s) are modeled.

11. And such cedar, tamarisk[?] (and) olive(-woods), bound up with red wool, as the *patili*-priest had placed on the woman, on the strap[?]—(now) these he takes away from her, and he places them with the *naḫiti*-loaf.

16. [And] the *patili*-priest gives a jug of wine to the woman, while she hands over to him two young goats. And them the woman "sacrifices" with wine,[12] and the *patili*-priest drives them away.

20. And when at the crossing of the road he arrives, then one young goat for the male [deities] of the *šinapši*[13] he [sac]rifices, and (the other) young goat for the male deities of the city he [sacri]fices.

24. [And] the [*pat*]ili-priest comes back, [and he be]fore (the door of[?]) the inner chamber bows down, (and) to the woman he [bow]s down, and he cries "well-being!" [And] they give to him to drink, [and] he goes forth.

29. The next morning[14] the woman washes. And if she is (shown) by a dream (to be) pure, then the *patili*-priest takes her in to the birth-stool.

33. And she bows down, and on the birth-stool places (her) hand.

35. But if she is (shown) by a dream (to be) impure, then she before the door of the inner chamber bows down. Further, out[side] she puts (her) hand forth toward the birth-stool. But when at night a

COMMENT: This text, of which fragments of six different copies have thus far been identified, deals with purificatory ceremonies performed on behalf of a woman. In the preserved lines, only the presence of the *harnau-*, "birth-stool," indicates that a birth is involved. It is likely that these ceremonies were to be carried out soon before this apparatus was employed in the actual birth, although it must be noted that no mention of the entering into labor is preserved. It is unfortunate that both the initial lines and the colophons of all of the exemplars have been lost, for it is there that one might find an explicit statement of purpose for this ritual. It is certain only that the ritual is concerned with the mother in the (immediate?) preparturition period, and that it centers about her purification and ritual introduction to the birth-stool. Presumably evils or impurities which might otherwise threaten the lives of mother and child during birth are here removed. Possibly the lost Col. iv dealt with the birth of the child and his purification.

NOTES:

[1] ABot 17, KUB VII 39, KBo XVII 64, 464/w and Bo 4879.

[2] The text of Col. i has not been well preserved in any of the duplicates. The numbering of the lines here follows that of the main text.

[3] The birth-stool (*harnau-*) is the apparatus employed for delivery in birth rituals of Hurrian origin. The birth-stool seems to have consisted of a bowl upon which the mother sat, two pegs which she grasped during delivery, and possibly several boards placed under the bowl. See F. Sommer and H. Eheloff, *Das hethitische Ritual des Pāpanikri von Komana* (Leipzig, 1924), pp. 3-4.

[4] A type of priest whose chief, but not sole, sphere of activity was that of birth. In no text is he directly involved with parturition, however, but only with the purificatory rites surrounding birth.

[5] A member of the duck family.

[6] *zurgi* here, as well as *habi, itkalziya* and *kulamušiya* in ii 19, are Hurrian words whose precise meanings are uncertain. *zurgi* seems to be an undesirable quality (e.g., "pollution?") whose removal is sought. *habi* is probably a site within the ritual area, and *itkalziya* and *kulamušiya* appear to designate states (e.g., "purity") which it is hoped to reach through the performance of the ritual.

[7] For the magical practice of binding with colored wool in Hittite texts, see G. Szabó, *THeth* 1, 95-100.

[8] The anointing of the head of the woman here is a rite marking her entrance into a special state of purity conducive to successful delivery. For anointing in the ancient Near East as indicative of entrance into a new or special social status, cf. the anointing of the kings of Israel, e.g., of David in 2 Samuel 5:3.

[9] A substance employed in purificatory rites. It probably plays an important role in several birth rituals because of its approximate homophany with *harnau-*, "birth-stool."

[10] Cultic functionaries whose diverse duties included ritual purification and the making of music.

[11] A Hurrian pastry.

[12] That is, she simulates their slaughter by pouring over them wine representing their blood. The actual sacrifice is later carried out by the *patili*-priest at the crossroads.

[13] A Hurrian word indicating a part of a temple.

[14] The duplicate ABoT 17 indicates that this is the third day of the ritual proceedings.

star [tw]inkles, then he (the *patili*-priest) [t]akes the woman in to the birth-stool.[15]   And she bows down
to the birth-stool, [and (her)] h[and] she places forth (on it).   And she goes forth.
42.   [And] the *patili*-priest [before] the inner chamber makes a [seal]ing.   [And a bi]rd the *patili*-priest
takes [for]th.   [. . .] on the road, at the cro[ss]ing, [. . .] . . . he [. . .] inner chamber [. . .]
he [b]ows down.[16]

CHARACTER: Fourteenth century text of Hurro-Luwian provenience, preserved in copies of fourteenth and thirteenth
century date.

Text 6. KBo V 1 (excerpt)[1]

The activities detailed in the preserved portions of Text 5 are designed in part to purify the birth-stool
in anticipation of its role in parturition.   If, in spite of this ritual preparation, the apparatus proved de-
fective when actually employed, this was naturally perceived as a bad omen, indicative of the displeasure
of some deity.   The tablet KBo V 1 deals with this very eventuality.   The introduction (i 1-6) reads:
"Papanikri, *patili*-priest of the land of Kummanni, says as follows: 'If a woman is (seated) upon the
birth-stool and the dish of the birth-stool is damaged, or a peg is broken—Then if the woman has not yet
given birth, but is (still) seated thereupon, then the boards[?] they open again.   But it (the birth-stool) is
no longer pure'."

There follows the ritual itself: The *patili*-priest removes the birth-stool and its accessories from the home
of the mother, pausing at the door of the house to burn birds for several deities (i 7-11).   The implements
are then carried to a *šinapši*[2], where the *patili*-priest sets them down outside in a virgin spot.   Here the
woman gives birth (i 12-14).

The remainder of this, the day of birth, and the two following days are taken up by an oracular inquiry
to determine the cause of the bad omen and by purificatory rites intended to remove this blemish.
These ceremonies, which take place both within and outside of the *šinapši* (i 18-57, ii 1-6) and in the
home of the mother (ii 7ff.), do not seem to be peculiar to the birth situation and thus may be passed
over.   We need note only that the child is purified on the evening of the third day (ii 5).

However, on the fourth night is performed a ceremony which is indeed of interest here: After an involved
seven course cultic meal in the home of the mother, at which the chief Hurrian deities Tešup and Hepat
are the divine guests, and where the human company is composed of *patili*-priests and *katra*-women in
addition to the family of the mother, we find (iii 51-iv 36):

iii 51.   . . . When the seventh dish arrives, then the *katra*-women unravel[?] a garment.
54.   And when they have finished unraveling[?] the garment, then red wool they gather up, and it on top
of the garment they place, thereby fashioning a ball of yarn[?].   Then the *patili*-priest takes water (and)
fine oil, and these things he carries forth (from the house).   And they wipe down a lamb—(its) mouth (and)
its feet he (the *patili*-priest) washes off.   Further, with the fine oil he anoints it, and the red wool onto
his feet he binds.   Then the ball of yarn[?] they wrap around its head.
iv 9.   Then the *patili*-priest takes the lamb in(to the house), and he swings it seven times over the seven
fires.   Then he places it on the knees of a *katra*-woman.   But another *patili*-priest lifts up a pot of water
and it into the wash basin he pours.
15.   Then they wash the lamb.   Further, he pours out the bath water before the deity.   But they adorn
the lamb, and they dress it in red garments.   But they put the helmet[?] on it, and the wreath they put on
it.   And his (i.e., of the child) bracelets (on its forelegs) and the anklet(s) on its (hind-)feet they put, and
they take it to the *šinapši*.
22.   The offerant (i.e., the mother) goes behind.   But when they arrive at the gate of the *šinapši*, then the
offerant sits down, and the *patili*-priest takes the lamb away from her, and to a pure place takes it away.
And he cries "well-being!"
27.   Then the offerant(s) go into the *šinapši*, and with a bird for *urnazhiya*[3] he offers.   And one bird he

[15]At this point two of the duplicates, ABoT 17 and KBo XVII 64, begin to diverge from the main text.

[16]Col. iv is represented only by the ends of several lines in the main text.

COMMENT: In the section of KBo V 1 quoted here, in a rite similar to that involving a goat in Text 3 Rev. 7'ff., a lamb is employed as a substitute for the new-born child. While in Text 3 the animal is ritually associated with the infant through being touched to his body, the same goal is here attained through the dressing of the lamb in the clothes of the child. The substitution of the lamb for the child is also accomplished through the placing of it on the knees of a *katra*-woman (iv 11). This action may be interpreted either as a ritual parody of the setting of the new-born on the knees of the father (see H. Hoffner, *JNES* 27 [1968], 199), or as a symbolic representation of the birth itself, with the *katra*-woman playing the role of the mother. In any case, the washing of the lamb in iv 15 and the pouring out of the bath water before a deity must be understood as reflecting a normal purificatory rite carried out on a human infant. The purifications of the child which are cursorily mentioned in ii 5 and iv 32 were probably of this sort.

NOTES:

[1]See F. Sommer and H. Ehelolf, *Das hethitische Ritual des Pāpanikri von Komana* (Leipzig, 1924).

[2]See above, Text 5, Note 13.

[3]A Hurrian word, probably indicating a state of well-being.

offers for well-being. Then the offerants go away to their own houses. But when it is morning, then they purify the child, and above him they pound a stick[?] (into the wall).

34. Meanwhile the day passes, and seven-strength (and) triple-strength beer[?] they libate.

CHARACTER: Thirteenth century copy of fourteenth century composition of Hurro-Luwian background.

Text 7. KBo XVII 65[1]

Obv. 1. [Thus says So-and-so[2]: I]f a woman becomes pregnant, and in the house she [. . .] (but) she does not (as yet) seat herself on the [birth-]stool . . . . [. . .] she comes and with *kunzigannahit*[3] cleanses herself. She[?] [. . . .]

5. [When the seventh month (of pregnancy) ar]rives, then the husband does not any longer "en[ter"] with his wife.[4] And [. . . i]n the seventh month performs the *mala*(-offering)[5] of pregnancy.

7. Furthe[r, such] . . . -offerings [as (are)] before [her]—them (the offerings) (s)he perform[s] completely [. . . .] And again[?] (s)he performs the *mala*(-offering). Further, the *uzi*[6] (and) *zurgi*[7] (-offerings) (s)he perform[s]. And (s)he (thus) bestows [purit]y.

10. The next mornin[g the seer] purifies [he]r [mouth] as follows: The seer into a beaker of fired cla[y . . . pours[?].] But [there]in he throws *harnai*.[8] And cedar, olive [(and) tamarisk[?](-woods) there]in he places. And she purifies her own mouth. But [when] he [meanwhi]le speaks in Hurrian—this (material is the contents of) a separate tablet.[9]

14. Further, it is [not] allowed for her [to go[?]] back [to her home[?].] If someone summons her, then she goes into the sec[lusion] hut[?]. But as is the re[gulation] of the clean[sing] and of the purification (of the material) of the birth-stool, even [now thes]e things are the same.

17. For her, eat[ing] *astauwar*[10] [during this time[?]] is [n]ot allowed. [And] she does [no]t ea[t] *tappi*.[10] Groun[d-up] cress she does [not e]at, (but rather) garden cress she eat[s] continually.[11] The *astauwar* [of] the woman [her] h[usband eats continually] (but) [ast]auwar the woman does not eat.

20. [If] her husband [is wi]th her, then h[e] too is washed pure. And when it is ti[me] to eat [. . .] a table for her husband [is re]quired, and [fo]r his wife one is (also) required. And a bowl for (each of) them is required. Certainly he is [i]n her presence, but the woman does not eat [wi]th him.

24. Both the [utensi]ls of wood and the utensils of fired clay, the stool and the bed—each new thing— [they] t[ake . . .] empty. But such utensils as are of bronze—they burn therein. [And they are taken back. And al]l these things they take. There is nothing (left over).

27. But when [the woman] gives birth, and while the seventh day (after birth) is passing, then they perform the *mala*(-offering) of the new-born [. . .] on th[at] seventh day. Further, i[f a male child is bor]n, in whatever month [he is bo]rn—whether [one day or] three [d]ays remain—

31. [then from tha]t month they count off.[12] And when [the third month arrives, then the] male [child] with *kunzigannahit* they cleanse. For [the seers are] expert with the *kunzigannahit*, [and it to . . . (some deity) th]ey offer.

34. But [if] a female child is born, [then] from that month they count off. [But] when [the fourth] month [ar]rives, then the female child with *kunzigannahit* [they] cl[ean]se.

37. But when (it is time for) the Festival [of the Wo]mb—(that is,) at the time when she gives birth— how they perform the festival—[it is per]formed [(according to) a *kurta*-tablet.[13]] And it is (from) Kizzuwatna.[14] And I (the scribe) [do not know] the festival orally [by heart, b]ut (rather) I will fetch it from there.

40. [Un]til[?] [. . .] is brought to an end, then they do not strike or battle anyone, [n]or do they sin against anyone . . . .

44. [But] at the time when [the woman] becomes pregnant, then the Mother-goddesses of the body back [to . . . they transport[?].] And how for them they perform the festival there—this (material is the contents of) a separate tablet. [. . .] but when the [. . .] of the days has come—this (material) too (is the contents of) a separate tablet.

COMMENT: This tablet has unfortunately been broken into many fragments, and large portions of the text have been lost. Thus it has been necessary to make extensive restorations in order to reach an understanding of the contents. The structure of the text is unusual—the opening paragraph of each side begins: "If a woman becomes pregnant," and several paragraphs on each side specifically mention the act of birth itself. This tablet seems to contain two versions of a ritual regimen for pregnancy and post-parturition, one on each side. (Note, however, that the actual birth is not dealt with in any detail here.) In the first several paragraphs of each side the events and ritual activities of pregnancy are presented in chronological order, and there then follow (as a sort of appendix) more specific instructions for particular events within the regimen. The present tablet probably represents a compilation of several earlier, closely related, tablets, which were in part copied exactly, without regard to the new context—note the remark "(The text is) finished" in Rev. 60, although four additional lines of text remain on the reverse, and at least eight more on the edge. This text constitutes the most extensive description yet discovered of Hittite practice in the area of pregnancy and birth, and its provisions have consequently shaped to a great degree the schema presented above on pp. 4-6.

NOTES

[1] With duplicate KUB XLIV 59.

[2] The author of the text, who was probably, but not certainly, a woman.

[3] A Hurrian word designating a purificatory material of unknown character.

[4] That is, he no longer engages in sexual intercourse with her.

[5] This poorly attested type of offering seems to be of Hurrian origin.

[6] Another Hurrian offering.

[7] See above, Text 5, Note 6.

[8] See above, Text 5, Note 9.

[9] See above, Text 2, Note 2.

[10] Foodstuffs of which nothing more specific is known.

[11] Apparently the woman is not allowed to eat wild cress, but only cress grown under (ritually?) controlled conditions.

[12] That is, in the calculation of the day after birth on which the ritual cleansing of the child is to be performed, an approximation is permitted.

[13] A type of wooden tablet.

[14] An area in southern Anatolia from which Hurro-Luwian culture was disseminated over all of the Hittite empire.

47. [While . . . a wo]man is pregnant, then for the Mother-goddesses of the body a monthly festival [they perform, then to them . . .] they also [gi]ve continually, and (on) the return trip they keep possession of them. But when [. . .] they [brin]g? them, then they place them in the house of the birth-stool. [. . .] the seers likewise give continually.

51. [If a woman gives birth,] then on whatever day she gives birth, for the Mother-goddesses [of the body and for Ḫepat . . . on th]at day the Festival of Birth [they perform . . . . And for th]em they complete the festival according to that model. [. . .] they send back here. To the Mother-goddesses and to Ḫepat [they sacrifice. And to . . .] they [sac]rifice—as much as (seems) good to the offerant.

Rev. 1. [Thus says So-and-so: If a woman becomes preg]nant, but does not (as yet) seat herself on the birth-stool, [. . .] the regulation is as follows:

3. [. . . wh]en for her in the sixth month two days remain, [then the husband does not any longer "en]ter" [with his wife.]

5. [. . .] the *maršaya*-offerings[15] of the Old Women [she performs . . . . Wh]en the *mala*(-offering) of Apritta[16] [she performs? . . . . F]urther, thereaf[ter] the *maršaya*-offerings of the seer she performs. [But when] the *maršaya*-offerings of the seer she completes, [then . . .] to the *adani*[17] an *uzi*(-offering) she performs completely. And they bestow purity.

10. [. . . the house] is whitewashed (and) sprinkled. And it has already been shut up.[18] [. . . tha]t woman (i.e., the practitioner) completes the rites. Whatever is before her, [. . .] and they give to her to eat. Whether it is of the Black Deity[19] [or o]f [. . .] the rites she completes.

14. [B]ut [when? of tha]t deity the praise [an]d well-being (-offerings) (are) before her, then [a]ll (this) [she do]es. And if for her certain offerings of the *šinapši*[20] are [establish]ed [by oracle] to be un-favorable?, then these things also she [per]forms.

17. But when she [bu]rns the bird[s], then whatever religious concern[21] [come]s? to be see[n] in a dream—when anything appears in her mind—then in regard to that matter [. . .] i[n] the *šinapši* she [bu]rns up the birds completely.

20. Further, in the *šinapši* [. . . for well-be]ing she offers. And she eats in the *šinap*[*ši*]. And the woman [com]es for[th] from the temple. But in front, in the gate, hot loaves are broken, and they mak[e] them into crumbs. [And] when the woman has come forth, one *šaniddu*-loaf[22] (and one) *gaz(za)mi*(-loaf)[22] they g[iv]e. And to the *pa*[*tili*-]priest,[23] the *katra*-women[24] (and) the torchbearers they giv[e] *gazzami*-loaves.

25. And the woman go[es] out to the inn. And she is washed pure. But if it (seems) good to her hus[ba]nd, then [he eats] with her. But wherever (seems) r[ight]—thither (s)he drives. But wh[e]n the eighth month arrives, and wh[en two days] remain, then the woman washes herself. [But] the next morning they wa[sh] her [mouth, and the uten]sils of fired clay and the utensils of wood—each of them empty—they ta[ke.] B[ut such utensils as are of bronz]e—they burn [there]in. And they are taken back. [And all these things they tak]e. There is [no]thing (left over).

31. [. . . A]nd the woman goes into that house. B[ut?] to? the birth-stool? . . . [. . . in th]ose rooms she performs the *zurgi*-offering. Further, she [. . .] throws in [*ḫarna*]*i*?. And cedar, olive [(and) tamarisk? (-woods) . . .] (s)he does not pla[ce in]side.

35. [And her own mouth she purif]ies. But how he meanwhile speaks in Hurrian—this (material is the contents of) a [sep]arate [tablet . . . .] and inside they cleanse. [A]nd the woman does not go forth again . . . .

38. [But (when) the woman gives birth, and whi]le the seventh day (after birth) is passing—then the *mala* (-offering) of the new-born on that seventh day [(s)he performs. And if a male child has been bo]rn, in whichever [mon]th he has been born—whether one day or two days [remai]n—then [from that mon]th they count off.

41. But when the third month a[rrives,] then the male child with *kunziganna*[*ḫit*] they [cl]eanse. For the seers are expert with the *kunzigannaḫit*, and it t[o . . . they of]fer.

43. But if a female child is born, [then from th]at month they cou[nt] off. But [wh]en the fourth month arrives, then they clean[se] the female child with [*kunzi*]*gannaḫit*.

45. But when (it is time for) [the Festival] of the Womb—(that is,) at the time when she [gi]ves birth—how they [per]form the festival—it is performed (according to) a *kurta*-tablet. And it is (from) Kizzuwatna. [And I] do not know the festival orally by heart, but (rather) they will bring [it] . . . from there.

¹⁵A type of offering found only in this text.

¹⁶A poorly attested goddess, perhaps of Hurro-Luwian origin.

¹⁷A Hurrian word designating a utensil employed in the cult.

¹⁸That is, the house is prepared for its cultic role through a purification consisting of the whitewashing of its walls and the sprinkling of water on its floor to settle the dust. It has also previously been sealed off to profane traffic.

¹⁹Probably an epithet of the Mood-god

²⁰See above, Text 5, Note 13.

²¹Literally, "whatever matter of the *šinapši*." For an incubation oracle, see Text 4, Col. iii 29ff. Here if any religious matter should reveal itself to the woman as unfulfilled, it must be expiated through a burning of birds in the *šinapši*.

²²Pastries.

²³See above, Text 5, Note 4.

²⁴See above, Text 5, Note 10.

47. If they [make off]ering to Ḥepat, then these things they take: one duck, [. . . so many] *mulati-*[loaves²²] of one-half handful of flour (each), five thin loaves, oil, a wooden [. . .] a little, and one jug of wine . . . (s)he offers. Further [. . .] (s)he fills.

50. Further, the seer [takes] two? [pieces of cloth–either . . .] or a shirt, or [. . . o]r a cur[tain?,] and [over the offerant he places (them).] But under her hands [he places] two thick loaves] of one handful of pap (each). But] below [her feet, two thick loaves] of one handful of pap (each) he places. But [on] her neck a yoke [. . . he places.] Under it two *kišri*²⁵ [. . .] two *tarpa*[*la*²⁵ of . . . -colored wool? **he places. And] the seer sits down on** (her) back . . . . [. . . And] a small needle? of silver–its weight (is) one *tarna*²⁶–[. . .] is stu[ck? . . .] he takes away.

57. [And the seer says to her: "You] have become the maidservant of Ḥepat, and of her the maidservant [you shall remain?! . . .] and (of Ḥepat) the temple, the command and custom you shall observe!" [. . . t]o the deity she bows down–whatever (are) the materials (for the ritual), this [she gives.] (The text is) finished.²⁷

CHARACTER: Middle Hittite compilation of several texts of Hurro-Luwian origin. The tablets themselves are probably also to be dated to this period.

[25]Woolen products often employed in rituals of the Hurro-Luwian group.

[26]A very small unit of weight. In one text a pastry made from one-half handful of grain is said to be equivalent to one weighing one *tarna*.

[27]Not translated here are the last four lines of the reverse of this tablet and the eight fragmentary lines of its left edge which present details of further offerings.